CHINESE COOKING

Photography by Peter Barry and Jean-Paul Paireault
Recipes by Lalita Ahmed, Carolyn Garner, Moyra Fraser
    and Frederic Lebain
Designed by Richard Hawke
Edited by Jillian Stewart

3256
This 1993 edition produced for Book Express, Inc.
Airport Business Center, 29 Kripes Road, East Granby, Connecticut, USA
Copyright © 1993 CLB Publishing Ltd, Godalming, Surrey, England
All rights reserved
Printed and bound in Hong Kong
USA direct sales rights in this edition are exclusive to Book Express, Inc.
ISBN 1-85833-023-8

CHINESE
COOKING

Book Express
Quality and Value in Every Book...

Contents

Introduction

Most of us will never travel to China, but we can enjoy the country's delicious and varied dishes without leaving our own kitchens. China is a vast country and its sheer size is one of the key elements in the success of this wonderful cuisine. Because of its great land area, China has a diverse range of climates and crops, hence a plethora of regional specialties.

In the South, the weather is warm and the meals light. Stir-fried dishes with crisp vegetables are popular and rice is the staple. It is this style that we are most familiar with in the West as most of the Chinese communities that have settled overseas are from this area. Canton in particular is at the heart of this tradition and many dishes such as stir-fried rice and sweet and sour dishes originated here. By contrast, the North is a cold, wheat growing region that has a hearty, warming cuisine. Noodles are eaten more often than rice, rich sauces and meat dishes are popular, as are pancakes and dumplings. It is from this area that the legendary Peking Duck originates.

In the East, the mild climate and fertile soil mean that both rice and wheat grow well and rice and noodles compete equally for popularity. Seafood and freshwater fish are very popular and here some of China's most popular fish – carp, shad, bream and perch – are found in abundance. Noodles combined with seafood or poultry are particular favorites in tea houses. In the western provinces it is strong spicy flavors which predominate rather than the fresh, light flavors of the East. Szechuan cuisine, with its spicy, hearty flavors has a growing number of devotees.

The techniques used in Chinese cooking are crucial to the final taste and look of a dish. Stir-frying is probably the most important Chinese cooking method and to this end a wok is best but a large heavy-based frying pan can be used. Some of the ingredients may not be familiar, but if you do not have a Chinese supermarket within easy reach there are easy alternatives readily available. Cooking Chinese food takes only minutes for most recipes, but preparation often involves much slicing and chopping, so it is best to have everything ready to go. Ingredients are generally cut to approximately the same size so that they cook in the same amount of time.

Chinese food is one of the most popular ways of dining out because it is simple, tasty and varied. Try bringing a taste of China into your cooking and with a bit of practice China will not be so far away.

NOODLES IN SOUP

A simple soup that is extremely tasty.

SERVES 4-6

---

1 lb small rounds of noodle cakes
Salt
6 cups chicken or beef broth, or
   thick stock
4 oz cooked shredded chicken
2 eggs, hard-cooked and sliced
4 oz Chinese napa cabbage, finely
   shredded (or iceberg lettuce)
2 green onions, thinly sliced

1. Cook the noodles in boiling, salted water for 5 minutes. Drain thoroughly.

2. Heat the broth or stock and add salt to taste. Put the cooked noodles in bowls, and pour the hot broth over them.

3. Garnish with chicken, sliced eggs, cabbage and green onions, and serve.

TIME: Preparation takes 10 minutes, cooking takes 6-8 minutes.

BUYING GUIDE: Noodles are available in different thicknesses – buy the thinest for soups.

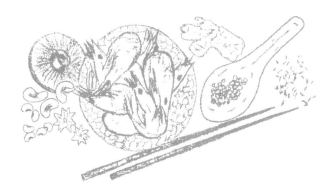

PEKING-STYLE SOUP

Duck stock is the basis of this tasty, filling soup, which contains meat and vegetables, and is delicately flavored with sesame seeds and soy sauce.

SERVES 4

4 slices smoked ham
1 head Chinese cabbage
3¾ cups duck stock
1 tbsp sesame seeds
Pinch chopped garlic
1 tbsp soy sauce
½ tsp white wine vinegar
Salt and pepper
1 egg yolk, beaten

1. Cut the ham into small, even-sized cubes.

2. Cut the Chinese cabbage into small pieces and simmer briskly for 10 minutes in the duck stock.

3. Stir in the sesame seeds, garlic, ham, soy sauce, vinegar, and salt and pepper to taste.

4. Simmer for 10 minutes over a gentle heat. Using a teaspoon, drizzle the beaten egg yolk into the soup. Serve immediately.

TIME: Preparation takes about 5 minutes, cooking takes approximately 20 minutes.

VARIATION: Replace the smoked ham with a different smoked meat.

WATCHPOINT: The smoked ham is likely to change color during cooking.

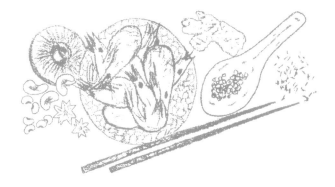

CRAB AND WATERCRESS SOUP

Crab and watercress make a great combination in this quick soup.

SERVES 4-6

6 cups chicken stock
4 oz white crabmeat, shredded
2 green onions, finely chopped
2 bunches watercress, finely chopped
Salt and freshly ground black pepper to
   taste
1 tsp cornstarch or arrowroot
1 tbsp water
2 tsps light soy sauce
A few drops sesame oil

1. Bring the stock to a boil with the crab-meat, onions, and watercress and simmer for 4-5 minutes. Add salt and pepper to taste.

2. Mix the cornstarch with the water and add to the soup. Allow to simmer gently for another 2 minutes, stirring occasionally.

3. Add soy sauce and sesame oil, mix well, and simmer for 2 minutes. Serve immediately.

TIME: Preparation takes 10 minutes, cooking takes 8-9 minutes.

BUYING GUIDE: Ensure the watercress is not limp – it deteriorates rapidly once it reaches the supermarket.

CURRY SOUP WITH MEATBALLS

A hearty soup that is perfect for heating up a cold winter night.

SERVES 4

Meatballs
8 oz lean ground beef
1 clove garlic, crushed
1 onion, peeled and finely chopped
½ tsp salt
½ tsp curry powder
½ tsp ground cinnamon
½ tsp ground cloves
½ tsp ground pepper
½ cup breadcrumbs
1 small egg, lightly beaten

Peanut oil

Broth
1 tsp garam masala
1 tsp turmeric
1 tsp curry powder
1 onion, peeled and finely chopped
2½ cups water
1 clove garlic, crushed
½ cup shredded coconut, soaked in 1
    cup hot water for 15 minutes

1. Mix together meatball ingredients, and form into small balls about the size of walnuts.

2. Heat wok, add oil and, when hot, fry meatballs. When browned well all over, remove with a slotted spoon, and drain on paper towels.

3. Carefully drain oil from wok. Add 1 tsp of oil, and fry spices for the broth for 30 seconds.

4. Add onion and garlic, and cook together for 3 minutes.

5. Meanwhile, strain coconut in a sieve, press out as much liquid as possible, and discard the pulp.

6. Add water and coconut milk to the wok and simmer together for 5 minutes.

7. Strain soup and return to wok. Add meatballs, adjust seasoning and simmer 5 minutes more. Serve hot.

TIME: Preparation takes 30 minutes, cooking takes 20 minutes.

Bamboo Shoot Soup

*A very decorative soup. Beaten egg sifted into the hot
soup gives a very special effect.*

SERVES 4

3 oz bamboo shoots, cut into thin
  matchsticks
4 dried Chinese black mushrooms, soaked
  for 15 minutes in warm water
3¾ cups chicken stock
1 tbsp wine vinegar
2 tbsps light soy sauce
Salt and pepper
½ tsp cornstarch, combined with a little
  water
1 egg
10 chives

1. Blanch the bamboo shoots in boiling,
salted water for 3 minutes. Rinse and set
aside to drain.

2. Cook the mushrooms in boiling, salted
water for 10 minutes. Rinse and set aside
to drain.

3. Bring the stock to the boil and add the
bamboo shoots, mushrooms, vinegar, and
soy sauce, and season with salt and
pepper to taste. Cook for 10 minutes.

4. Stir in the cornstarch and bring the soup
slowly back to the boil.

5. Reduce the heat. Beat the egg
thoroughly. Place the beaten egg in a
strainer and add to the soup by shaking
back and forth over the hot soup.

6. Add the chives to the soup and serve
piping hot.

TIME: Preparation takes about 5 minutes, cooking takes approximately 30 minutes.

WATCHPOINT: Make sure the soup is boiling hot before adding the beaten egg.

COOK'S TIP: Try to buy fresh chives for this soup, as they have a
much better flavor than dried chives.

TURKEY SOUP WITH BLACK MUSHROOMS

This unusual blend of flavors makes a tasty, warming soup.

SERVES 4

---

6 oz turkey breast meat
1 tbsp sesame oil
2 oz dried Chinese black mushrooms,
   soaked for 15 minutes in warm water
3¾ cups chicken stock
1 tbsp soy sauce
1 slice fresh ginger
Salt and pepper

---

1. Cut the turkey meat into thick slices and then into small cubes.

2. Heat the sesame oil in a wok and stir-fry the meat until brown. Remove from the pan and drain off any excess oil.

3. Cook the mushrooms in boiling, salted water for 10 minutes. Rinse and drain well.

4. Place the mushrooms in a saucepan with the stock. Stir in the meat, soy sauce, ginger, and salt and pepper to taste.

5. Bring to the boil and then simmer gently for 15 minutes.

6. Remove the slice of ginger just before serving. Serve the soup very hot.

TIME: Preparation takes about 8 minutes, cooking takes approximately 35 minutes.

SERVING IDEA: Sprinkle the soup with 1 tbsp chopped fresh chives before serving.

WATCHPOINT: Don't forget to remove the slice of ginger before serving.

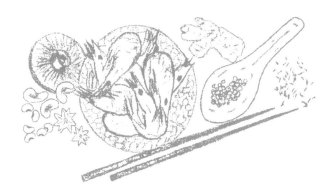

CORN AND CHICKEN SOUP

A classic soup that is still a great favorite.

SERVES 4

1 medium-sized chicken, with giblets
8 oz can creamed corn
1 onion, peeled and coarsely chopped
1 carrot, scraped and coarsely chopped
1 stick celery, chopped
6 peppercorns
Parsley stalks
1 bay leaf
4 cups water
Salt
Pepper

Garnish
Chopped parsley or chives

1. Clean chicken, and cut into quarters. Put into wok with giblets, chopped vegetables, peppercorns, bay leaf, parsley stalks, seasoning, and water.

2. Bring to a boil. Reduce heat and simmer for 30 minutes. Strain and return stock to wok.

3. Discard the vegetables and giblets. Remove meat from chicken and cut into fine shreds.

4. Add undrained corn to stock, and bring to a boil. Simmer for 5 minutes.

5. Add chicken and cook for 1 minute.

6. Sprinkle with chopped parsley or chives. Serve hot.

TIME: Preparation takes 15 minutes, cooking takes 45 minutes.

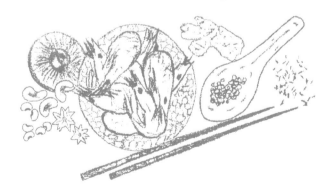

CRAB SOUP WITH GINGER

*This delicately flavored soup, with fresh crab and a
hint of ginger, is perfect for serving at a special dinner.*

SERVES 4

1 carrot, chopped
1 onion, chopped
½ leek, chopped
1 bay leaf
2 medium-sized crabs
3¾ cups fish stock
1-inch piece of fresh ginger, chopped
1 tsp Sake Japanese wine (optional)
Salt and pepper

1. Make a vegetable stock by putting the carrot, onion, leek, and bay leaf into a saucepan with a large quantity of water. Bring to the boil and add the crabs. Allow to boil briskly for 20 minutes or until cooked.

2. Remove the crabs when cooked and allow to cool. Once cooled, break off the pincers and break the joints, cut open the back and open the claws. Carefully remove all the crab meat.

3. Bring the stock to the boil and add the ginger, Sake and the crabmeat. Boil for 15 minutes.

4. Check the seasoning, adding salt and pepper as necessary. Serve very hot.

TIME: Preparation takes about 40 minutes, cooking takes approximately 35 minutes. It takes about 30 minutes for the crab to cool, before you can comfortably remove the meat with your fingers.

WATCHPOINT: Allow plenty of time for opening the crab and removing all the meat. If time does not permit preparing fresh crab, use canned crabmeat.

COOK'S TIP: Prepare the soup the day before serving. If allowed to rest overnight, the flavor of the soup will develop deliciously. Reheat gently just before serving.

SHRIMP FU YUNG

This dish is perfect for lunch or an evening snack.

SERVES 4-6

Oil
1-2 cloves of garlic, chopped
4 oz shrimp, peeled
4 oz green beans, sliced
1 carrot, shredded
6 eggs
Salt and freshly ground black pepper to
    taste
Sauce
1 cup chicken stock
¼ tsp salt
2 tsps soy sauce
1 tsp sugar
1 tsp cornstarch

1. Heat 2 tbsps oil in a wok. Add the garlic and stir-fry for 1 minute.

2. Add the shrimp and stir-fry for 1 minute.

3. Add the beans and carrots and stir-fry for 2 minutes. Remove and keep on one side.

4. Beat the eggs with salt and pepper to taste, and add the cooled shrimp mixture.

5. Clean the wok and heat 1 tsp oil. Pour 4 tbsps of the egg mixture and cook like a pancake. When the egg is set, turn the pancake over and cook on the other side until lightly golden. Place on a warm platter and keep warm. Repeat until all the egg mixture is used.

6. To make the sauce, beat the stock with the other sauce ingredients and stir over a gentle heat until the sauce thickens. Serve the pancakes with this sauce.

TIME: Preparation takes 10 minutes, cooking takes 4 minutes for filling and 3-4 minutes for each pancake.

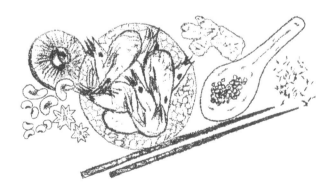

THE PEKING DUCK

A magnificent recipe much loved by all fans of Chinese cooking.

SERVES 6

---

1 duck, weighing 4 lbs
1 short American cucumber
4 green onions

Sauce
Small can yellow bean sauce
3 tbsps sugar
2 tbsps oil

---

1. Clean and dry the duck.

2. Finely shred the cucumber and green onions.

3. Preheat the oven to 400°F. Place the duck on a grill rack set on top of a baking pan. Cook the duck for 1½ hours. The skin should be very dark and crispy, if it is not, turn the heat up and cook for a further 10 minutes.

4. For the sauce, heat 2 tbsps oil in a small pan. Add the yellow bean paste and sugar. Cook together for 1-2 minutes.

5. Peel the skin off the duck and cut into 2-inch slices. Serve on a heated platter.

6. Carve the meat off the duck into 2-inch slices, serve on a separate platter accompanied by the sauce.

TIME: Preparation takes about 15 minutes, cooking takes approximately 2 hours.

SERVING IDEA: The duck skin and meat are eaten by wrapping them in pancakes which are first of all brushed with a teaspoon of sauce and a layer of cucumber and green onions.

COOK'S TIP: The pancakes can be bought ready-made in delicatessens or supermarkets.

RICE PAPER SHRIMP PARCELS

The perfect nibble for a cocktail party.

MAKES ABOUT 20 PARCELS

8 oz shrimp, shelled and de-veined
1 egg white
½ tsp cornstarch
2 tsps dry sherry
1 tsp sugar
1 tsp light soy sauce
6 green onions, finely sliced
Salt
Pepper
⅔ cup peanut oil
1 packet rice paper

1. Dry the prepared shrimp on paper towels.

2. Mix egg white, cornstarch, wine, sugar, soy sauce, green onions and seasonings together. Mix in shrimp.

3. Heat peanut oil in wok until hot.

4. Wrap five or six shrimp in each piece of rice paper.

5. Gently drop in rice paper parcels and deep-fry for about 5 minutes. Serve hot.

TIME: Preparation takes 15 minutes, cooking takes 15 minutes.

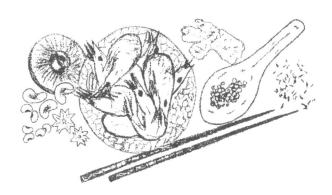

SCRAMBLED EGGS WITH SHRIMP

Fish-flavored scrambled eggs, cooked with shrimp.

SERVES 4

12 shrimp, peeled
8 eggs, beaten
½ stick celery, diced small
1 green onion, chopped
1 tsp fish sauce
Salt and pepper

1. Cut the shrimp into small pieces.

2. Stir the shrimp into the eggs and add the celery, green onion, and fish sauce.

3. Season with pepper, and a little salt if necessary.

4. Cook by stirring over a gentle heat. When cooked to your liking, serve immediately.

TIME: Preparation takes about 10 minutes, cooking takes approximately 10 minutes.

WATCHPOINT: The fish sauce is very salty. Taste the scrambled eggs after they have cooked before adding any more salt.

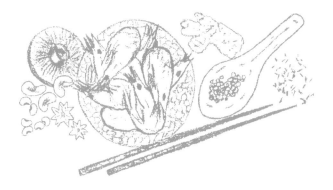

SZECHUAN BANG BANG CHICKEN

This is a good dish to serve as an appetizer.

SERVES 2

2 chicken breasts
1 European cucumber

Sauce
5 tbsps peanut butter
2 tsps sesame oil
½ tsp sugar
¼ tsp salt
2 tsps stock
½ tsp chili sauce

1. Simmer the chicken in a pan of water for 30 minutes. Remove the chicken breasts and cut them into ½-inch thick strips.

2. Thinly slice the cucumber. Spread cucumber on a large serving platter. Pile the shredded chicken on top.

3. Mix the peanut butter with the sesame oil, sugar, salt, and stock. Heat the sauce over a gentle heat until warm.

4. Pour the sauce over the chicken and sprinkle the chili sauce evenly over the top.

TIME: Cooking takes about 30 minutes, final preparation takes 5 minutes.

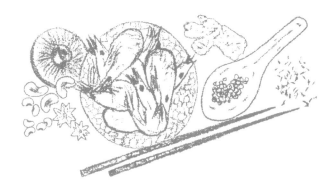

SESAME SHRIMP TOASTS WITH CRISPY SEAWEED

Have great fun trying to eat crispy seaweed with your chopsticks!

SERVES 2-4

4 oz pork fat
6 oz cooked shrimp
1 egg white
Salt and pepper to taste
1 tbsp cornstarch
2 slices white bread
7 tbsps sesame seeds
Oil for deep frying

Crispy Seaweed
2 lbs greens
4 tbsps slivered almonds
Oil for deep frying
½ tsp salt
1½ tsps sugar

1. With a very sharp knife, cut the greens into the finest shreds possible. Dry by spreading them out on paper towels for half an hour.

2. Finely chop pork fat and shrimp. Blend together well with egg white, salt, pepper, and cornstarch. Spread the "paste" thickly on the slices of bread. Remove the crusts.

3. Sprinkle the paste thickly with sesame seeds, pressing them on well.

4. Heat the oil. Lower one slice of bread at a time into the hot oil, spread side down, for 2 minutes. Turn over and fry the other side for 30 seconds. Repeat for other slice of bread.

5. Cut each shrimp toast in half, then into finger-sized strips. Set aside and keep warm.

6. Deep fry, or shallow fry the almonds until golden. Drain well.

7. Heat the oil until it is about to smoke. Remove from the heat for 30 seconds.

8. Add all the shreds of greens. Stir and return pan to the heat and fry for 2-3 minutes. Remove and drain well.

9. Serve the shrimp toasts and crispy seaweed on a well heated platter, sprinkle crispy seaweed evenly with salt, sugar, and almonds.

TIME: Preparation takes 10 minutes for the shrimp toasts and 5 minutes for the seaweed, cooking takes about 10 minutes for the shrimp toasts and about 3 minutes for the crispy seaweed.

Seafood Chow Mein

Chinese noodles cooked with mussels, clams, and
vegetables and served in a rich ginger
and wine flavored sauce.

SERVES 4

8 oz Chinese noodles
½ green pepper, seeded
½ red pepper, seeded
1 tbsp oil
½ tsp chopped garlic
½ tsp chopped fresh ginger
½ green onion, chopped
5 oz uncooked mussels (shelled)
2 oz uncooked clams (shelled)
1 tbsp Chinese wine
2 tbsps soy sauce
Salt and pepper

1. Cook the noodles in boiling, salted water. Rinse them under cold water and set aside to drain.

2. Cut the peppers into thin slices.

3. Heat the oil in a wok and stir-fry the garlic, ginger, peppers, and green onion for 1 minute.

4. Stir in the mussels, clams, Chinese wine, soy sauce, and the cooked noodles.

5. Mix together well, using chopsticks. Season with salt and pepper and cook for 4-5 minutes or until cooked through completely.

TIME: Preparation takes about 15 minutes, cooking takes approximately 15 minutes.

VARIATION: Add other types of seafood to this dish.

WATCHPOINT: In Step 5 heat the noodles thoroughly, turning them in the sauce to coat evenly.

SZECHUAN FISH STEAK

Szechuan food is hot and this recipe makes a wonderfully zippy fish dish.

SERVES 4

1½ lbs haddock
2 tsps salt
2 tbsps cornstarch
1 egg

Sauce
1 large onion
2 cloves garlic
3 slices fresh ginger
2 chili peppers
2 slices Szechuan Ja Chai pickle (see Cook's Tip)
1 dried chili
Oil for deep frying
7 tbsps chicken stock
3 tbsps soy sauce
2 tbsps tomato paste
2 tbsps hoisin sauce
1 tbsp sugar
1 tbsp wine vinegar
2 tbsps dry sherry

1. Cut fish into 2 x 1-inch oblong pieces. Rub with salt. Blend the cornstarch with the egg. Dip the fish in the egg mixture to coat on both sides.

2. Thinly slice the onion. Finely chop the garlic, ginger, chilies, pickle, and dried chili.

3. Heat 4 tbsps oil in a large frying pan. Add the onion and other chopped vegetables and stir-fry for 2 minutes.

4. Add the stock, soy sauce, paste, hoisin sauce, sugar, vinegar, and sherry. Stir over a high heat until well reduced.

5. Heat about 4 cups oil in a deep fryer. When hot, add the fish and fry for 2 minutes. Remove and drain.

6. Place them in the pan of sauce. Simmer in the sauce for 5 minutes before serving.

TIME: Preparation takes 10 minutes, cooking takes 10 minutes.

COOK'S TIP: If you cannot obtain the Ja Chai pickle, substitute your favorite hot pickle.

STEAMED SHRIMP

*Fresh shrimp, garnished with zucchini peel, steamed
and served with a fish-flavored sauce.*

SERVES 4

1 tbsp fish sauce
1 tbsp water
1 tbsp wine vinegar
1 tbsp soy sauce
2 tsps sugar
10 fresh mint leaves, finely chopped
1 shallot, chopped
Salt and pepper
12 fresh shrimp, peeled and cleaned
2 medium-sized zucchini, peeled and
　 the peel cut into long strips

1. Mix together the fish sauce, water,
vinegar, soy sauce, sugar, mint, shallot,
and salt and pepper. Stir well and set
aside for a least 1 hour.

2. Just before serving time, season the
shrimp with plenty of salt and pepper.

3. Roll the strips of zucchini peel around
the shrimp and cook them in a Chinese
steamer for 5 minutes.

4. Serve the shrimp piping hot,
accompanied by the sauce.

TIME: Preparation takes about 20 minutes and 1 hour standing time for the sauce. Cooking
takes about 10 minutes for 2 batches.

COOK'S TIP: If the strips of zucchini peel are not very pliable, blanch them in boiling
water for 3 seconds before wrapping around the shrimp.

WATCHPOINT: The sauce can be prepared just before cooking the shrimp,
but it is much tastier if prepared at least 1 hour in advance.

HONEY SESAME SHRIMP

Shrimp sweetened with honey and sprinkled
with sesame seeds – the perfect dish to spoil yourself with.

SERVES 4

1 cup all-purpose flour
Pinch of salt
Pepper
1 egg, lightly beaten
⅔ cup water
1 lb shrimp, shelled and de-veined
2 tbsps cornstarch
Oil for deep frying
1 tbsp sesame oil
2 tbsps honey
1 tbsp sesame seeds

1. Sift flour and salt and pepper into a bowl. Make a well in the center, add egg and water, and gradually mix in the flour.

2. Beat to a smooth batter and set aside for 10 minutes.

3. Meanwhile, toss shrimp in cornstarch and coat well. Shake off any excess cornstarch. Add shrimp to batter and coat well.

4. Heat oil in wok and add shrimp, a few at a time. Cook until batter is golden. Remove shrimp, drain on paper towels, and keep warm. Repeat until all shrimp have been fried.

5. Carefully remove hot oil from wok. Gently heat sesame oil in pan.

6. Add honey and stir until mixed well and heat through. Add shrimp to mixture and toss well.

7. Sprinkle over sesame seeds and again toss well. Serve immediately.

TIME: Preparation takes 20 minutes, cooking takes 20 minutes.

CRISPY FISH WITH CHILI

Choose your favorite white fish for this recipe.

SERVES 4

1 lb fish fillets, skinned, bones removed, and cut into 1-inch cubes

Batter
½ cup all-purpose flour
1 egg, separated
1 tbsp oil
6 tbsps milk
Salt
Oil for deep frying

Sauce
1 tsp grated ginger
¼ tsp chili powder
2 tbsps tomato paste
2 tbsps tomato chutney
2 tbsps dark soy sauce
2 tbsps Chinese wine or dry sherry
2 tbsps water
1 tsp sugar

1 red chili, seeds removed, and sliced finely
1 clove garlic, crushed
Salt
Pepper

1. Sift the flour with a pinch of salt. Make a well in the center, and drop in the egg yolk and oil.

2. Mix to a smooth batter with the milk, gradually incorporating the flour. Beat well. Cover and set aside in a cool place for 30 minutes.

3. Whisk egg white until stiff, and fold into batter just before using.

4. Heat oil in wok. Dip fish pieces into batter and coat completely. When oil is hot, carefully lower fish pieces in until cooked through and golden brown – about 10 minutes. Remove with a slotted spoon.

5. Reheat oil and refry the fish pieces for 2 minutes. Remove with a slotted spoon and drain on paper towels.

6. Carefully remove all but 1 tbsp of oil from the wok.

7. Heat oil, add chili, ginger, garlic, chili powder, tomato paste, tomato chutney, soy sauce, sugar, wine and water, and salt and pepper to taste.

8. Stir well over heat for 3 minutes. Increase heat and toss in fish pieces. Coat with sauce and, when heated through, serve immediately.

TIME: Preparation takes 40 minutes, cooking takes 30 minutes.

Stewed Chicken and Pineapple

Pineapple complements the chicken wonderfully in this dish.

SERVES 2-3

Marinade
2 tbsps light soy sauce
1 tbsp oil
1 tbsp cornstarch
1 tsp salt
½ tsp sesame oil
2 tbsps water

1½ lbs boneless chicken breast, cut into cubes

Sauce
1½ tsps cornstarch
1 cup water or chicken stock
2 tsps dark soy sauce
Salt to taste

2 tbsps oil
1 onion, peeled and cut into chunks
2 green onions, finely chopped
1 inch fresh ginger, peeled and thinly sliced
4-5 pineapple rings, cut into chunks

1. Mix the marinade ingredients together.

2. Add the cubed chicken and marinate for 10-12 minutes.

3. Mix the sauce ingredients together in a bowl.

4. Heat the oil in a wok and fry the onions for 2 minutes until just tender. Add the drained chicken and fry for 3-4 minutes.

5. Add the ginger and fry for 1 minute.

6. Add any remaining marinade and the sauce ingredients and bring to the boil. Cook, stirring, until the sauce thickens then add the pineapple chunks. Heat through. Remove from the heat and serve immediately.

TIME: Preparation takes 30 minutes, cooking takes 15 minutes.

SOY CHICKEN WINGS

These delicious chicken wings can be served on any occasion.

SERVES 4

2 lbs chicken wings
½ tsp crushed ginger
1 tbsp light soy sauce
1 tbsp sugar
1 tsp cornstarch
2 tsps sesame oil
2 tbsps dry sherry
Salt
Pepper
2 tbsps peanut oil
2 green onions, sliced
1 tbsp dark soy sauce
1 star anise
3 tbsps water

1. Wash chicken wings and dry on paper towels.

2. Mix together ginger, light soy sauce, sugar, cornstarch, sesame oil, wine, and seasoning. Pour marinade over chicken wings and leave for at least 1 hour, turning occasionally.

3. Heat peanut oil until very hot. Add green onions and chicken wings, and fry until chicken is browned well on all sides.

4. Add dark soy sauce, star anise, and water. Bring to the boil, and simmer for 15 minutes.

5. Remove star anise. Serve hot or cold.

TIME: Preparation takes 10 minutes, plus 1 hour for the chicken to marinate. Cooking takes 20 minutes.

CHICKEN AND CASHEW NUTS

A popular combination that works extremely well.

SERVES 4

12 oz boneless chicken breast, sliced into
   1-inch pieces
1 tbsp cornstarch

Marinade
1 tsp salt
1 tsp sesame oil
1 tbsp light soy sauce
½ tsp sugar

Oil for deep frying
1 cup cashew nuts
2 green onions, chopped
1 small onion, peeled and cubed
1 inch fresh ginger, peeled and sliced
2 cloves of garlic, sliced
3 oz snow peas
2 oz bamboo shoots, thinly sliced

Sauce
2 tsps cornstarch
1 tbsp hoisin sauce
¾ cup chicken stock
Pinch monosodium glutamate (optional)

1. Roll the chicken pieces in cornstarch.
Discard the remaining cornstarch.

2. Mix the marinade ingredients together
and pour over chicken. Leave to stand for
10 minutes.

3. Heat oil for deep frying and fry cashew
nuts until golden brown. Remove the nuts
and drain on paper towels.

4. Heat 2 tbsps oil in a wok and stir-fry
the onions, ginger, and garlic for 2-3
minutes.

5. Add snow peas and bamboo shoots and
stir-fry for 3 minutes. Remove the fried
ingredients.

6. Add 1 tbsp oil to the wok and fry the
chicken for 3-4 minutes. Remove the
chicken.

7. Clean the wok and add a further 2 tsps
oil and return chicken, cashew nuts and
fried vegetables to the wok.

8. Prepare the sauce by mixing the
cornstarch, hoisin sauce, chicken stock,
and monosodium glutamate together.

9. Pour over the chicken. Mix well and
cook until the sauce thickens and
becomes transparent.

TIME: Preparation takes 15 minutes, cooking takes 15 minutes.

VARIATION: A few chunks of pineapple will add extra zest to the dish.

STEAMED CHICKEN

*A great method of cooking chicken and
one which brings out all its flavor.*

SERVES 3-4

1½ lbs boneless chicken

Marinade
1 tbsp light soy sauce
1 tsp brown sugar
1 tsp salt
1 tbsp cornstarch
2 tbsps oil
½ tsp monosodium glutamate (optional)

4 oz dried mushrooms, soaked in boiling
    water for 5 minutes and sliced, or
    ordinary mushrooms
½ inch fresh ginger, peeled and sliced
4 green onions, finely chopped
2 tbsps stock or water, if needed

1. Cut the chicken into 1-inch pieces. Mix the marinade ingredients together and mix with the chicken. Leave to marinate for 15 minutes.

2. Place a plate in a steamer and put the chicken, mushrooms, ginger, half the onion, and the stock on top. Steam over boiling water for 15-20 minutes.

3. Serve with the remaining onions sprinkled over the chicken. The steaming can also be done on a greased lotus leaf or a banana leaf. The flavor is quite stunning.

TIME: Preparation takes 15 minutes, plus 15 minutes to marinate the chicken. Cooking takes 15-20 minutes.

COOK'S TIP: If you can obtain dried mushrooms do use them as their flavor is far superior to ordinary mushrooms.

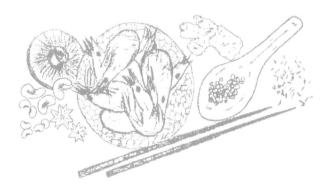

ROAST CRISPY DUCK

This dish can be served as a main course for 4 or as an appetizer for 6.

SERVES 4-6

4½ lbs duck or goose, prepared for
    cooking
4 tbsps corn syrup
1 cup water
12 green onions, cut into 2-inch lengths
½ tsp red food coloring
2 tbsps tomato paste

Duck Dip
½ cup sugar
4 tbsps sweet bean paste
2 tbsps sesame oil
½ cup water

---

1. Wash the duck and pat it dry on a clean cloth. Ease the finger between the skin and flesh of the duck, starting at the neck end and working the length of the bird. Put a stick or large skewer through the neck and the cavity of the duck to wedge it securely. This will make the duck easier to handle. Hold the duck over the sink and pour boiling water all over it. Pat the duck dry.

2. Melt half the corn syrup and dissolve in the water. Stand the duck on a rack over a deep tray. Slowly pour the corn syrup liquid over the duck 3 or 4 times. Leave the duck in the refrigerator for 6-8 hours, or overnight, until the skin is dry.

3. Remove the skewer. Stand the duck on a rack in a roasting pan. Preheat the oven to 400°F and cook for 30 minutes. Turn over and cook the underside for a further 30 minutes.

4. Melt the remaining corn syrup with the tomato paste and add the food coloring. Spread over the duck and cook for a further 30 minutes. (The duck should have a crisp, reddish-brown skin.)

5. Heat the wok and add the mixed ingredients for the duck dip. Cook for 3-4 minutes until the sugar has dissolved and the dip is smooth. Serve in individual cups.

6. Remove the duck skin in squares. Slice the duck flesh and serve with the skin on top.

TIME: Preparation takes 15-20 minutes, plus 6-8 hours to dry, cooking takes 1 hour 30 minutes.

SLICED DUCK WITH BAMBOO SHOOTS AND BROCCOLI

*A delightful recipe that mixes some of
China's best-loved ingredients.*

SERVES 2

2¼ lb small duck
1 tsp monosodium glutamate (optional)
2½ tsps cornstarch
2 tbsps water
4 oz broccoli, chopped
3 tbsps oil
2-3 green onions, chopped
1 inch fresh ginger, peeled and thinly
    sliced
1 clove garlic, peeled and finely chopped
4 oz bamboo shoots, sliced
½ tsp sugar
Salt and freshly ground black pepper to
    taste
¼ cup chicken stock
2 tsps rice wine or sweet sherry
Few drops sesame oil

1. Cut the duck flesh into bite-size pieces,
removing all the bones.

2. Mix the the monosodium glutamate,
1½ tsps cornstarch, and 1 tbsp water
together. Stir into the duck. Marinate for
20 minutes.

3. Cook the broccoli in boiling water for 1
minute. Drain thoroughly.

4. Heat the wok and add the oil. Stir-fry
the onions, ginger, garlic, and bamboo
shoots for 1-2 minutes.

5. Add the duck pieces and stir-fry for 2-3
minutes. Add the sugar, salt and pepper to
taste, stock, rice wine, sesame oil, and
broccoli. Stir-fry for 3 minutes.

6. Add the remaining cornstarch and water
blended together. Stir over the heat until
the sauce thickens. Serve immediately.

TIME: Preparation takes 5 minutes, plus 20 minutes for the duck to marinate. Cooking
takes approximately 10 minutes.

COOK'S TIP: Fresh root ginger keeps well if tightly wrapped in
plastic wrap and stored in the refrigerator.

DEEP-FRIED CRISPY CHICKEN

Everybody loves fried chicken and this recipe is especially tasty.

SERVES 4

3-4 lbs chicken, prepared for cooking

Seasoning
1 tsp salt
½ tsp five-spice powder
1½ oz corn syrup
2 tbsps malt vinegar
1 cup white vinegar
Oil for deep frying

1. Wash the chicken and hang it up by a hook to drain and dry. The skin will dry quickly. Pour boiling water over the chicken 4-5 times, to partially cook the skin. This will make the skin crisp during frying. Rub salt and five-spice powder well inside the chicken cavity.

2. Dissolve the corn syrup and vinegars in a pan over a gentle heat. Pour over the chicken. Repeat several times, catching the solution in a drip tray.

3. Leave the chicken to hang and dry for 1½-2 hours, until the skin is smooth and shiny.

4. Heat the oil for deep frying. Deep-fry the chicken for 10 minutes. Ladle hot oil carefully over the chicken continually, until the chicken is deep brown in color. (The skin puffs out slightly.)

5. Cook for a further 3-4 minutes and remove from the oil. Drain on paper towels. Cut into small pieces and serve with a dip.

TIME: Preparation takes approximately 1 hour, plus 1½-2 hours for drying the duck. Cooking takes 13-14 minutes.

CHICKEN AND BEAN SPROUT SALAD

Steamed chicken and bean sprouts, coated in a refreshingly light sauce.

SERVES 4

3 cups bean sprouts
12 oz boneless chicken breast
1 tbsp soy sauce

Sauce
2 tbsps chopped chives
1 tbsp white wine vinegar
1 tsp sugar
1 tbsp soy sauce
Pinch chopped garlic
1 tbsp peanut oil
½ tsp sesame oil
Salt and pepper

1. Cook the bean sprouts for 2 minutes in boiling water. Drain and refresh under cold water. Set aside to drain completely.

2. Sprinkle the chicken with 1 tsp soy sauce and cook in a Chinese steamer.

3. Once the chicken is cooked, set it aside to cool and then slice thinly.

4. Prepare the sauce by mixing together the remaining ingredients and seasoning with a little salt and pepper. Allow the sauce to stand for 20 minutes.

5. Mix together the bean sprouts and the chicken. Pour over the sauce and serve.

TIME: Preparation takes about 15 minutes, cooking takes about 15 minutes.

VARIATION: The chicken could be cooked in stock, to which the soy sauce has been added.

COOK'S TIP: Mix together the sauce ingredients the day before using them. The flavors will have more time to develop fully.

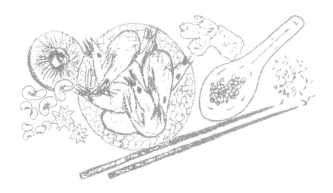

SZECHUAN CHILI CHICKEN

If you like chilies this is sure to become a favorite.

SERVES 3-4

¾ lb boneless chicken breast, cooked
1 tsp salt
1 egg white
⅓ cup oil
1½ tbsps cornstarch
2 slices fresh ginger
2 small dried chili peppers
2 green or red peppers
2 fresh chili peppers
2 tbsps soy sauce
2 tbsps wine vinegar

1. Cut the chicken into bite-sized pieces. Add the salt, egg white, 1 tbsp oil, and cornstarch. Mix and rub these evenly over the chicken pieces to form a thin coating.

2. Chop the ginger and dried chili. Cut the peppers into bite-sized pieces.

3. Heat the remaining oil in a wok. Add the ginger and chili peppers and stir-fry for 1 minute.

4. Add the chicken pieces, separating them while stirring. Add the peppers, soy sauce, and vinegar, and fry for a further 2 minutes.

5. Serve immediately with rice.

TIME: Preparation takes 5 minutes, cooking takes 5 minutes.

COOK'S TIP: Vary the amount of chili peppers according to how hot you like your food!

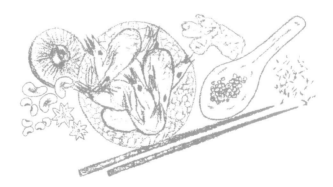

PORK WITH GREEN PEPPERS

A quickly-prepared stir-fried pork dish with
green peppers and a hoisin-based sauce.

SERVES 4

1 lb pork fillet
2 tbsps oil
½ tsp chopped garlic
2 green peppers, seeded and cut into thin
    matchsticks
1 tsp wine vinegar
2 tbsps chicken stock
1 tbsp hoisin sauce
Salt and pepper
1 tsp cornstarch, combined with a little
    water

1. Slice the pork thinly, then cut into narrow strips. Heat the oil in a wok. Add the garlic, green pepper, and the pork. Stir together well. Cook for 1 minute, shaking the wok occasionally.

2. Stir in the vinegar, stock, and hoisin sauce. Season to taste with salt and pepper. Cook for 3 minutes.

3. Stir in the cornstarch and cook, stirring continuously, until the desired consistency is reached.

TIME: Preparation takes about 10 minutes, cooking takes 5 minutes.

VARIATION: Replace the green pepper with a red one.

WATCHPOINT: It is not necessary to add sugar to this sauce as the hoisin sauce is sweet enough.

BEEF WITH GREEN PEPPER AND CHILI

*The classic mix of beef and green pepper is
given extra punch by the addition of chili peppers.*

SERVES 4

---

1 lb fillet of beef, cut into 1-inch strips

Marinade
2 tbsps dark soy sauce
1 tsp sesame oil
Pinch baking soda
¼ tsp ground black pepper
½ tsp salt

Oil for cooking
2 green peppers, seeded and thinly sliced
1 onion, peeled and sliced
2 green onions, chopped
1 inch fresh ginger, peeled and sliced
2 garlic cloves, peeled and chopped
3 green chilies, sliced

Sauce
2 tbsps chicken stock
½ tsp monosodium glutamate (optional)
1 tsp dark soy sauce
Salt to taste
Few drops sesame oil

1. Marinate beef with the marinade ingredients for 15 minutes.

2. Heat 2 tbsps oil and stir-fry green pepper and onions for 2 minutes. Remove to a plate.

3. Reheat wok, add 2-3 tbsps oil and fry ginger, garlic, and green chilies for 1 minute.

4. Add beef and stir-fry for 4-5 minutes. Add sauce ingredients, mixed together, and the fried peppers and onions. Stir-fry for a further 2 minutes, remove ginger slice and serve.

TIME: Preparation takes 15 minutes, plus 15 minutes for the beef to marinate. Cooking takes 10-12 minutes.

STIR-FRY BEEF WITH MANGO SLICES

This oriental combination of ingredients is refreshingly different.

SERVES 2-3

½ lb fillet of beef
1 tbsp cooking wine
1 tbsp soy sauce
1 tsp cornstarch
¼ tsp sugar
¼ tsp pepper
1 large mango
4 tbsps oil
1 tbsp shredded ginger
1 tbsp shredded green onions

1. Cut beef into thin bite-sized slices. Marinate in the wine, soy sauce, cornstarch, sugar, and pepper for 20 minutes.

2. Skin mango, cut into ¼-inch thick slices.

3. Set wok over a high heat, pour 4 tbsps oil into the wok, wait until it's almost smoking. Reduce heat to moderate, stir-fry the beef and ginger for 1-2 minutes. Remove with a slotted spoon.

4. Toss the mango slices in the hot oil for a few seconds, return the beef and ginger, and add the green onions. Stir over the heat for a further few seconds. Serve immediately.

TIME: Preparation takes 10 minutes, plus 20 minutes for the mest to marinate. Cooking takes about 3 minutes.

COOK'S TIP: If you cannot get a fresh mango – canned mango is available from supermarkets.

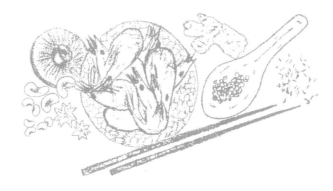

MEAT AND SHRIMP CHOW MEIN

*This chow mein is a wonderful mix
of vegetables, meat, and seafood.*

SERVES 4

1 lb dried Chinese noodles or broken
   spaghetti
¼ cup oil
2-3 green onions, chopped
4 oz cooked ham, shredded
¾ cup peeled shrimp
4 oz shredded carrots
4 oz green beans, sliced
Salt to taste
1 tsp sugar
1 tbsp rice wine or dry sherry
4 oz cooked chicken, shredded
2 cups bean sprouts
2½ tbsps soy sauce

1. Cook the noodles in boiling, salted water for 4-5 minutes. Rinse under cold water and drain thoroughly.

2. Toss in 1 tbsp oil. Heat the remaining oil in a wok.

3. Add the onions, ham, shrimp, carrots, and green beans and stir-fry for 2-3 minutes.

4. Add the salt, sugar, wine, chicken, and bean sprouts. Cook for 2 minutes.

5. Add the cooked noodles and soy sauce. Cook for 1-2 minutes. Serve immediately.

TIME: Preparation takes 20 minutes, cooking takes 12-15 minutes.

SPICED BEEF

A classic recipe which requires the best-quality beef.

SERVES 2-3

Marinade
1 tsp sugar
2-3 star anise, ground
½ tsp ground fennel
1 tbsp dark soy sauce
¼ tsp monosodium glutamate (optional)

1 lb fillet of beef, cut into 1-inch strips
1 inch fresh ginger, peeled and crushed
½ tsp salt
2 tbsps oil
4 green onions, sliced
½ tsp freshly ground black pepper
1 tbsp light soy sauce

1. Mix the marinade ingredients together.

2. Add the beef strips, ginger, and salt, and marinate for 20 minutes.

3. Heat the oil in wok and stir-fry the onions for 1 minute.

4. Add the beef, ground pepper, and soy sauce and stir-fry for 4-5 minutes.

TIME: Preparation takes 10 minutes, plus 20 minutes for the beef to marinate. Cooking takes 5-6 minutes.

COOK'S TIP: Fresh ginger keeps well if wrapped in cling wrap and stored in the refrigerator.

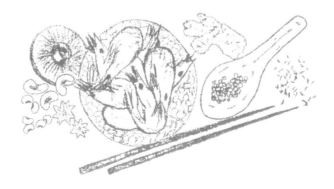

FILLET STEAK CHINESE STYLE

Fillet steak is best for this quick-fry recipe.

SERVES 4

8 oz fillet or rump steak, cut into 1-inch
    pieces
Pinch of baking soda
1 tbsp light soy sauce
1 tsp sesame oil
2 tsps dry sherry
2 tsps sugar
1 tsp cornstarch
Salt
Pepper
2 tbsps dark soy sauce
4 tbsps water
2 tbsps peanut oil
2 cloves garlic, crushed
2 green onions, sliced diagonally into
    ½-inch pieces
½ tsp crushed ginger
1 can straw mushrooms, drained
1 can baby corn, drained
1 tbsp oyster sauce

Garnish
Green onion flowers (cut green onions
into 2 inch lengths. Carefully cut into fine
shreds, keeping one end intact, and then
soak in ice cold water until curling)

1. Put steak in a bowl and sprinkle over baking soda.

2. Mix together light soy sauce, sesame oil, wine, half the sugar, half the cornstarch, and seasoning. Pour over the steak and leave for at least one hour, turning meat occasionally.

3. Meanwhile, make sauce by mixing 2 tbsps of dark soy sauce, remaining sugar and cornstarch, and water. Mix together and set aside.

4. Heat wok, add peanut oil and, when hot, fry steak for 4 minutes. Remove from wok and set aside.

5. Add garlic, green onions, ginger, mushrooms, baby corn, and finally steak.

6. Add oyster sauce and mix well. Add sauce mixture and bring to the boil. Cook for 3 minutes, stirring occasionally.

7. Serve hot with rice, garnished with green onion flowers.

TIME: Preparation takes 15 minutes, plus 1 hour for the meat to marinate. Cooking takes 20 minutes.

Pork Spare Ribs

A great restaurant favorite which tastes just as good made at home.

SERVES 4

16-20 spare ribs
1 tsp salt
Oil
1 tsp ginger paste
1 tsp garlic paste
1 tsp onion paste
Pinch monosodium glutamate (optional)
1 tsp light soy sauce
1 tsp cornstarch
1 egg
½ tsp Shao Hsing wine or dry sherry
½ tsp chili oil

Sauce
3 tbsps sugar
3 tbsps vinegar
1 tbsp tomato catsup (optional)
1 tsp cornstarch
1 tsp water
1 tbsp dark soy sauce
½ tsp salt
½ tsp freshly ground black pepper

1. Trim excess fat from spare ribs and rub with salt. Add 4 tbsps oil to the wok and fry the ginger, garlic, and onion for 1-2 minutes. Add the spare ribs and stir-fry for 6 minutes.

2. Remove to a dish and add the monosodium glutamate, light soy sauce, cornstarch, egg, wine, and chili oil. Marinate for 10 minutes.

3. Prepare the sauce by mixing all the sauce ingredients together in the wok and bringing them gently to the boil. Simmer for 2-3 minutes and add the spare ribs along with their marinade. Stir fry until the liquid is reduced to half its original quantity.

4. Put all the ingredients onto a roasting pan and spread out evenly. Bake at 375°F for 25 minutes. Baste occasionally with the liquid from the tray and oil. The spare ribs should have browned well and be well coated with seasoning. Serve hot or cold.

TIME: Preparation takes 25 minutes, cooking takes 40-45 minutes.

Sweet and Sour Beef

*The combination of sweet and sour is an
old favorite for Chinese food lovers.*

SERVES 2

Batter
1 cup all-purpose flour
1½ tsps baking powder
4 tbsps cornstarch
4 tbsps oil
8 oz fillet of beef, cut into 1-inch cubes
1 onion, peeled and cut into wedges
1 inch fresh ginger, peeled and thinly
    sliced
1 clove garlic, peeled and crushed
1 green pepper, seeded and chopped

Sweet and Sour Sauce
4 tbsps sugar
¼ tsp salt
4 tbsps red wine vinegar
1 tsp fresh ginger, peeled and minced
6 tbsps water
1 tbsp cornstarch or arrowroot
2 tsps cooked oil
Few drops food coloring
Oil for deep frying

1. For the batter: sieve the flour, baking
powder and cornstarch.

2. Beat in 1 tbsp oil and add sufficient
water to make a thick, smooth batter.

3. Heat 3 tbsps oil in a wok and stir-fry
the beef for 2 minutes. Remove the beef
and set aside.

4. Fry the onion, ginger, garlic, and green
pepper for 2-3 minutes in the same oil.
Remove the wok from the heat.

5. Mix the sauce ingredients together and
add to the wok. Return the wok to the
heat and bring to the boil gently. Lower
the heat and simmer gently for 2-3
minutes until thick and clear.

6. Meanwhile, dip the beef cubes into the
batter and deep fry in the hot oil until
golden brown and crisp.

7. Drain on paper towels. Arrange in a
deep dish and pour the hot sauce over the
beef. Serve with a chow mein dish or fried
rice.

Time: Preparation takes 15 minutes, cooking takes 15 minutes.

Variation: Thinly sliced carrots, cucumber, and zucchini may also be
added along with the onion, ginger, and green pepper.

STEAMED LAMB WITH MUSHROOM SAUCE

A great combination that should please most appetites.

SERVES 4-6

2¼ lbs boned leg of lamb, cut
    into strips
2 green onions, thinly sliced
Salt and freshly ground black pepper
2 tsps oil
2 cloves of garlic, peeled and sliced
1 tsp cornstarch
Pinch monosodium glutamate (optional)
5 tbsps light soy sauce
3 tbsps rice wine or dry sherry
1 tsp crushed black pepper
1 inch fresh ginger, peeled and
    thinly sliced
1 cup sliced mushrooms
Few drops sesame oil

1. Put the lamb into a saucepan and add sufficient water to cover. Boil 5 minutes. Drain the lamb and retain the water. Arrange lamb strips in a deep dish and sprinkle the green onions on top. Season with pepper and salt.

2. Heat the oil in a wok and fry the garlic until brown. Remove the garlic and discard.

3. Mix together the cornstarch, monosodium glutamate, soy sauce, wine, crushed pepper, ginger, and 4 tbsps reserved water.

4. Stir the cornstarch mixture into the oil in the wok, add the mushrooms, and cook for 1-2 minutes. Pour over the lamb.

5. Cover the lamb with overlapping foil and tie around the rim. Put the dish in a steamer and steam over boiling water for 2 hours. Serve with the sesame oil sprinkled over the lamb.

TIME: Preparation takes 20-25 minutes, cooking takes 2 hours 10 minutes.

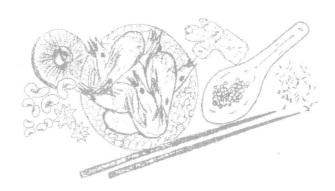

SWEET AND SOUR PORK

This really needs no introduction because of its popularity.
The dish originated in Canton, but is reproduced
in most of the world's Chinese restaurants.

SERVES 2-4

1 cup all-purpose flour
4 tbsps cornstarch
1½ tsps baking powder
Pinch salt
1 tbsp oil
Water
8 oz pork fillet, cut into ½-inch cubes

1 onion, sliced
1 green pepper, seeded, cored and sliced
1 small can pineapple chunks, juice
    reserved
Oil for frying

Sweet and Sour Sauce
2 tbsps cornstarch
½ cup light brown sugar
Pinch salt
½ cup cider vinegar or rice
    vinegar
1 clove garlic, crushed
1 tsp fresh ginger, grated
6 tbsps tomato catsup
6 tbsps reserved pineapple juice

1. To prepare the batter, sift the flour, cornstarch, baking powder, and salt into a bowl. Make a well in the center and add the oil and enough water to make a thick, smooth batter. Using a wooden spoon, stir the ingredients in the well, gradually incorporating flour from the outside, and beat until smooth.

2. Heat enough oil in a wok to deep-fry the pork. Dip the pork cubes one at a time into the batter and drop into the hot oil. Fry 4-5 pieces of pork at a time and remove them with a draining spoon to paper towels. Continue until all the pork is fried.

3. Pour off most of the oil from the wok and add the sliced onion, pepper, and pineapple. Cook over high heat for 1-2 minutes. Remove and set aside.

4. Mix all the sauce ingredients together and pour into the wok. Bring slowly to the boil, stirring continuously until thickened. Allow to simmer for about 1-2 minutes or until completely clear.

5. Add the vegetables, pineapple, and pork cubes to the sauce and stir to coat completely. Reheat for 1-2 minutes and serve immediately.

TIME: Preparation takes about 15 minutes, cooking takes about 15 minutes.

VARIATION: Use beef or chicken instead of the pork. Uncooked, peeled shrimp can be used, as can whitefish, cut into 1-inch pieces.

PORK WITH BLACK BEAN SAUCE

A tasty recipe which brings together classic Chinese ingredients.

SERVES 2-3

8 oz lean pork, cut into 1-inch cubes
1 tbsp oil
1 red pepper, cored, seeds removed, and
　　sliced

Marinade
3 tbsps black soya beans, rinsed in cold
　　water and crushed with back of a spoon
2 tbsps dry sherry
1 tsp grated ginger
2 tbsps light soy sauce
3 cloves garlic, crushed
1 tbsp cornstarch
½ cup water

1. Mix together black beans, wine, ginger, soy sauce, and garlic.

2. Blend cornstarch with 2 tbsps of water and add to mixture.

3. Place pork in a bowl, and pour over marinade. Toss together well. Leave for at least 30 minutes.

4. Heat wok, add oil and stir-fry red pepper for 3 minutes. Remove and set aside.

5. Add pork, reserving marinade. Stir-fry pork until browned well all over.

6. Add marinade and remaining water. Bring to the boil. Reduce heat, cover, and gently simmer for about 30 minutes, until pork is tender, stirring occasionally. Add more water if necessary.

7. Just before serving, add red pepper and heat through. Serve with plain white rice.

TIME: Preparation takes 40 minutes, cooking takes 45 minutes.

BUYING GUIDE: Black soya beans are available from health food stores.

FIVE-SPICE BEEF WITH BROCCOLI

A traditional recipe boosted by the addition of five-spice powder.

SERVES 2

8 oz fillet or rump steak
1 clove garlic, crushed
½ tsp finely grated ginger
½ tsp five-spice powder
2 tbsps peanut oil
4 oz broccoli florets
Bunch of chives, snipped into
    1-inch lengths
½ tsp salt
1 tbsp dark soy sauce
¾ cup hot water
2 tsps cornstarch, mixed with 1 tbsp cold
    water

1. Cut steak into thin slices, then into narrow strips. Mix together with garlic, ginger, and five-spice powder.

2. Heat wok, add 1 tbsp of oil, and stir-fry broccoli for 4 minutes.

3. Remove broccoli and add remaining oil.

4. Add meat, and stir-fry for 3 minutes.

5. Add broccoli, soy sauce, salt, and water, and heat to simmering point.

6. Mix cornstarch with cold water, and pour into wok, stirring continuously until liquid thickens.

7. Toss in chives, stir, and serve immediately with boiled rice.

TIME: Preparation takes 15 minutes, cooking takes 15 minutes.

SZECHUAN EGGPLANT

An unusual side-dish which adds extra spice to meals.

SERVES 2

Oil
1 large eggplant cut into 2-inch long and
  ½-inch thick strips
3 cloves garlic, peeled and finely sliced
1 inch fresh ginger, peeled and
  shredded
1 onion, peeled and finely chopped
2 green onions, chopped
4 oz cooked and shredded chicken
1 red or green chili, cut into strips

Seasoning
½ cup chicken stock
1 tsp sugar
1 tsp red wine vinegar
½ tsp salt
½ tsp freshly ground black pepper

Sauce
1 tsp cornstarch
1 tbsp water
1 tsp sesame oil

1. Heat the wok and add 3 tbsps oil. Add eggplant and stir-fry for 4-5 minutes. The eggplant will absorb a lot of oil; keep stirring or else they will burn. Remove from wok and put to one side.

2. Heat the wok and add 2 tbsps oil. Add the garlic and ginger and fry for 1 minute.

3. Add the onions and fry for 2 minutes. Add the chicken and chili. Cook for 1 minute.

4. Return the eggplants to the wok. Add the blended seasoning ingredients and simmer for 6-7 minutes.

5. Stir in the blended sauce ingredients and simmer until the sauce thickens. Serve with extra sesame oil if desired.

TIME: Preparation takes 15 minutes, cooking takes 18-20 minutes.

COOK'S TIP: Vary the spiciness of this dish by increasing the quantity of chilies.

Stir-Fried Sticky Rice

*Glutinous rice cooked with stir-fried mushrooms,
ginger, and green onions.*

SERVES 4

9 oz medium-grain rice
2 tbsps oil
2 green onions, chopped
½ onion, chopped
1 slice fresh ginger
4 dried Chinese black mushrooms, soaked
   for 15 minutes in warm water, drained
   and sliced
Salt and pepper

1. Wash the rice in plenty of cold water
and place it in a sieve. Pour 5½ cups
boiling water over the rice.

2. Heat the oil in a wok and fry the green
onions, onion, and ginger until golden
brown.

3. Add the mushrooms and continue
cooking, stirring and shaking the wok
frequently.

4. Add the rice and stir well. Pour over
enough water to cover the rice by ½ inch.

5. Cover and cook over a moderate heat
until there is almost no liquid left. Reduce
the heat and continue cooking until all the
liquid has been absorbed. This takes
approximately 20 minutes in total.

6. Add salt and pepper to taste, remove
the slice of ginger, and serve immediately.

TIME: Preparation takes 5 minutes and cooking takes approximately 25 minutes.

VARIATION: Replace the water with beef stock to give the rice more flavor.

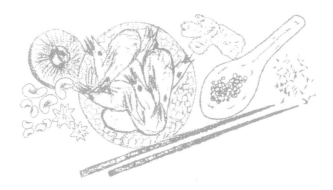

VEGETABLE STIR-FRY

*A marvellous blend of Chinese vegetables and nuts,
stir-fried in a little oil and then cooked in an aromatic sauce.*

SERVES 4

2 dried lotus roots, soaked overnight in
   water
2 tbsps oil
1½ cups bean sprouts
½ red pepper, seeded and finely chopped
½ green pepper, seeded and finely
   chopped
½ green onion, chopped
1 head Chinese cabbage, finely chopped
3 oz dried Chinese black mushrooms,
   soaked for 1 hour in warm water
1 zucchini, thinly sliced
¾ cup frozen peas
2 tbsps cashew nuts, roughly chopped
1 tsp sugar
2 tbsps soy sauce
1¾ cups chicken stock
Salt and pepper

1. Cook the lotus roots in boiling, lightly salted water for 20 minutes. Slice thinly.

2. Heat the oil in a wok and stir-fry, in the following order, the bean sprouts, peppers, onion, Chinese cabbage, lotus root, mushrooms, zucchini, peas and cashew nuts.

3. Stir in the sugar, soy sauce, and stock.

4. Season with salt and pepper and cook for 30 minutes, stirring frequently.

5. Serve the vegetables slightly drained of the sauce.

TIME: Preparation takes about 10 minutes, cooking takes approximately 35 minutes.

VARIATION: Any type of nut could be used in this recipe, for example, walnuts, hazelnuts, or almonds.

COOK'S TIP: If time permits, this recipe is even more delicious if the vegetables are stir-fried separately, each cooked vegetable being removed from the wok before continuing with the next. Finish by cooking all the vegetables together for 30 minutes in the chicken stock as above.

Plain Fried Rice

*Producing perfect rice is a must
for lovers of Chinese food.*

SERVES 4

1 lb long grain rice
¼ tsp monosodium glutamate
2 tbsps oil
Salt

1. Wash the rice in 4-5 changes of cold water. Drain the rice and put into a large pan or wok. Add sufficient cold water to come 1-inch above the level of the rice. Bring to the boil.

2. Stir once and reduce the heat to simmer. Cover and cook gently for 5-7 minutes until the water has been totally absorbed and the rice is separate and fluffy, with the necessary amount of stickiness to be handled by chopsticks.

3. Spread the rice out on a tray to cool. Sprinkle with the monosodium glutamate. Heat the oil in wok or large frying pan and add the rice. Stir fry for 1-2 minutes.

4. Add salt to taste and stir-fry for a further 1-2 minutes.

TIME: Preparation takes 5 minutes, plus cooling time, cooking takes 10-11 minutes.

STIR-FRIED RICE WITH PEPPERS

*Long grain rice stir-fried with red and
green peppers, onions, and soy sauce.*

SERVES 4

6 oz long grain rice
1 tbsp peanut oil
1 onion, chopped
1 green pepper, seeded and cut into small
   pieces
1 red pepper, seeded and cut into small
   pieces
1 tbsp soy sauce
Salt and pepper
1 tsp sesame oil

1. Cook the rice in boiling water, drain
and set aside.

2. Heat the oil in a wok and stir-fry the
onion, add the peppers and fry until
lightly browned.

3. Add the rice to the wok, stir in the soy
sauce and continue cooking until the rice
is heated through completely.

4. Season with salt, pepper, and the
sesame oil, and serve.

TIME: Preparation takes 5 minutes, cooking takes approximately 25 minutes.

VARIATION: If you like the strong flavor of sesame oil, stir-fry the
vegetables and rice in this instead of the peanut oil.

WATCHPOINT: Do not overcook the rice in Step 1, or it will become sticky in Step 3.

FRIED VEGETABLES WITH GINGER

*Use your imagination with this recipe and adapt it
to whatever greens you can buy.*

SERVES 4-6

2¼ lbs mixed green vegetables
  (cabbage, spinach, kale, broccoli,
  bok choy and so on)
2 oz snow peas
1 tsp baking soda
2 tsps sugar
1 tsp salt
2 tbsps oil
1 inch fresh ginger, peeled and
  shredded
1 green pepper, seeded and diced
1 green or red chili, sliced into strips

Sauce
2 tsps dark soy sauce
1 tsp sugar
1 cup chicken stock
2 tsps cornstarch
1 tsp five spice powder

To Serve
½ tsp sesame oil
Freshly ground black pepper to taste

1. Cut greens into 3-inch pieces. Bring a large pan of water to the boil and add the sugar and salt.

2. Add the snow peas and greens and cook for 4-5 minutes. Drain green vegetables and discard water.

3. Add 1 tbsp oil to the vegetables and keep covered. Heat the remaining oil in the wok and stir-fry the ginger for 1 minute.

4. Add the green pepper and chilies and stir-fry for 10-12 minutes. Add the blended sauce ingredients and stir well. Simmer gently for 3-4 minutes.

5. Add the green vegetables and cook for 1 minute. Serve immediately, sprinkled with sesame oil and pepper.

TIME: Preparation takes 10 minutes, cooking takes 13-15 minutes.

KIWI AND COCONUT DUO

*Incredibly simple to prepare, this recipe is a delicious
blend of kiwi fruit, fresh coconut, and coconut milk.*

SERVES 4

4 kiwi fruit
1 fresh coconut
A little sugar (optional)

1. Remove the stalks from the ends of the kiwis.

2. Peel them lengthwise with a small sharp knife.

3. Slice them thinly widthways.

4. Cut the coconut into pieces, reserving all the milk.

5. Cut the coconut flesh into very thin slices.

6. Arrange the kiwi slices on a serving plate and surround with the slices of coconut.

7. Add a little sugar to the coconut milk if desired and pour over the fruit. Serve chilled.

TIME: Preparation takes about 25 minutes.

VARIATION: Coconut milk can now be bought in cans. It is usually of very high quality and is thicker than fresh coconut milk.

COOK'S TIP: The addition of sugar to the milk is optional, and depends upon the acidity of the milk.

SPUN FRUITS

*Often called toffee fruits, this sweet consists of fruit
fried in batter and coated with a thin, crisp caramel glaze.*

SERVES 4

Batter
1 cup all-purpose flour, sifted
Pinch salt
1 egg
½ cup water and milk, mixed half and half
Oil for deep frying

Caramel Syrup
1 cup sugar
3 tbsps water
1 tbsp oil

1 large apple, peeled, cored, and cut into
  2-inch chunks
1 banana, peeled and cut into 1-inch pieces
Ice water

1. To prepare the batter, combine all the batter ingredients, except the oil for deep frying, in a liquidizer or food processor and process to blend. Pour into a bowl and dip in the prepared fruit.

2. In a heavy-based saucepan, combine the sugar with the water and oil and cook over very low heat until the sugar dissolves. Bring to the boil and allow to cook rapidly until a pale caramel color.

3. While the sugar is dissolving, heat the oil in a wok and fry the batter-dipped fruit, a few pieces at a time.

4. While the fruit is still hot and crisp use chopsticks or a pair of tongs to dip the fruit into the hot caramel syrups. Stir each piece around to coat evenly.

5. Dip immediately into ice water to harden the syrup and place each piece on a greased dish. Continue cooking all the fruit in the same way.

6. Once the caramel has hardened and the fruit has cooled, transfer to a clean serving plate.

TIME: Preparation takes about 25 minutes, cooking takes from 10-15 minutes.

VARIATION: Litchis may be used. Organisation is very important for the success of this dish. Have the batter ready, syrup prepared, fruit sliced, and ice water on hand before beginning.

WATCHPOINT: Watch the syrup carefully and do not allow it to become too brown. This will give a bitter taste to the dish.

MELON SALAD

*A refreshing fruit salad, especially tasty
served after a heavy meal of many courses.*

SERVES 4

1 large cantaloupe melon
1 mango
4 canned litchis
4 large or 8 small strawberries
Litchi syrup from the can

1. Peel and seed the melon and cut into thin slices.

2. Peel and pit the mango and cut into thin slices.

3. Using a melon baller, cut as many balls as possible out the strawberries.

4. Arrange the melon slices evenly on 4 small plates.

5. Spread a layer of mango over the melon. Place a litchi in the center of each plate and arrange a few strawberry balls around the edges.

6. Divide the litchi syrup evenly between the plates of fruit and chill them in the refrigerator before serving.

TIME: Preparation takes about 30 minutes.

VARIATION: Use a honeydew melon instead of the cantaloupe variety.

COOK'S TIP: This dessert is best served well chilled from the refrigerator, so prepare it several hours in advance of serving.

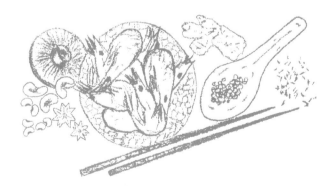

HALF-MOON BANANA PASTRIES

These crunchy pastries are rather dry, and are
traditionally served with a cup of Chinese tea.

SERVES 4

Dough
½ cup margarine
1 lb all-purpose flour, sifted
Pinch salt
½ cup water

Filling
3 bananas
2 tsps sugar
Pinch cinnamon
Few drops of lemon juice
1 egg yolk, beaten

1. Cut the margarine into the flour and salt. Using your fingers, incorporate the water gradually to form a ball. Wrap a damp cloth around the dough and leave it to rest in a cool place for 30 minutes.

2. Peel and crush the bananas with a fork. Add the sugar, cinnamon and lemon juice. Mix together well.

3. Roll out small pieces of dough on a lightly floured surface and cut into circles. Place a little of the banana filling on each round of dough. Fold into half-moon shapes and seal the edges first by pinching together with your fingers and then by decorating with a fork.

4. Continue until all the dough and filling have been used.

5. Brush the beaten egg yolk over the half-moon pastries. Pierce the pastries once to allow steam to escape during cooking. Cook in a moderate oven, 350°F, for approximately 20 minutes, until crisp and golden.

TIME: Preparation takes about 25 minutes, resting time for the dough is 30 minutes, cooking takes approximately 20 minutes.

VARIATION: Make up the pastries using different fruit fillings.

COOK'S TIP: The cooked dough in this recipe is very crisp. Serve the pastries with a fruit drink in summer and hot Chinese tea in winter.

WATCHPOINT: Be sure to seal the edges of the pastries thoroughly so that no filling escapes during cooking.

CANDIED APPLES

Candied fruit recipes are popular in Chinese cuisine.
This one is extra special with a rich batter, and
delicious sesame seeds to garnish.

SERVES 4

3 cooking apples
Flour for dipping
4 cups fresh oil
1¾ cups sesame oil
½ cup sugar
1 tbsp toasted sesame seeds

Batter
2 eggs
3 tbsps flour
3 tbsps cornstarch
Ice water

1. Peel and core the apples and cut into thick circles.

2. Mix the batter ingredients together to make a smooth, thick batter, adding water as necessary.

3. Dip the apples in flour and then into the batter.

4. Mix the two oils together and heat to moderate. Deep-fry the apples slices for about 1 minute. Drain and set aside.

5. Heat the oil until it is hot, then fry the apple slices again, for about 40 seconds. This will make them nice and crisp.

6. Pour off most of the oil used to fry the apples, leaving about 3 tablespoons. Add the sugar to this and stir over high heat until the sugar caramelizes. Add the apple slices and sesame seeds, stir to coat evenly and then remove.

7. Dip the slices into ice cold water to set the syrup before serving.

TIME: Preparation takes about 10 minutes, cooking takes 5 minutes.

EXOTIC FRUIT SALAD

Fresh fruit marinated in orange and litchi juice with just a hint of almond.

SERVES 4

1 papaya
1 pomegranate
2 kiwi fruit
4 rambutan fruit
4 canned litchis, plus the juice from the can
3 oranges
3 drops bitter almond extract, or ordinary
    almond extract

1. Peel all the fruit except the oranges, removing pips or pitting each fruit as necessary. Try to buy a fully ripe papaya for the salad. Cut it in half. Using a small spoon, remove all the pips and any stringy skin around them. Peel each half, but not too thickly as the flesh immediately below the skin is very good. Finally, cut the flesh into thin slices or other fancy shapes.

2. Peel two of the oranges. Remove all the pith and cut the flesh into small pieces.

3. Squeeze the juice from the remaining orange, mix this with the canned litchi juice and add the almond extract.

4. Cut all the remaining fruit into slices, rounds, or small cubes and combine these with the prepared papaya and oranges in a bowl. Pour over the almond flavored juices and leave the salad to marinate for a few hours in the refrigerator.

5. Serve chilled.

TIME: Preparation takes about 1 hour and the salad should be left to marinate for at least 3 hours.

SERVING IDEA: Cut a few fresh mint leaves into thin strips to garnish the fruit salad just before serving.

WATCHPOINT: Exotic fruit often arrives in the shops before it is ripe. The solution is to sweeten the sauce slightly before marinating the fruit in order to eliminate acidity.

BUYING GUIDE: If you cannot obtain the rambutan fruit, substitute more litchis.

Index

Photography by Peter Barry and Jean-Paul Paireault
Recipes by Lalita Ahmed, Carolyn Garner, Moyra Fraser
and Frederic Lebain
Designed by Richard Hawke